Serving from the Heart

2 CORINTHIANS

New Community Bible Study Series

Old Testament
> Exodus: Journey toward God
> 1 and 2 Samuel: Growing a Heart for God
> Nehemiah: Overcoming Challenges
> Psalms Vol. 1: Encountering God
> Psalms Vol. 2: Life-Changing Lessons
> Daniel: Pursuing Integrity

New Testament
> Sermon on the Mount 1: Connect with God
> Sermon on the Mount 2: Connect with Others
> The Lord's Prayer: Praying with Power
> Parables: Imagine Life God's Way
> Luke: Lessons from Jesus
> Acts: Build Community
> Romans: Find Freedom
> 2 Corinthians: Serving from the Heart
> Philippians: Run the Race
> Colossians: Discover the New You
> James: Live Wisely
> 1 Peter: Stand Strong
> 1 John: Love Each Other
> Revelation: Experience God's Power

JOHN ORTBERG

WITH KEVIN & SHERRY HARNEY

New Community

KNOWING. LOVING. SERVING. CELEBRATING.

Serving from the Heart

2 CORINTHIANS

WILLOW
Willow Creek Resources

ZONDERVAN.com/
AUTHORTRACKER
follow your favorite authors

ZONDERVAN®

2 Corinthians: Serving from the Heart
Copyright © 2008 by Willow Creek Association

Requests for information should be addressed to:

Zondervan, Grand Rapids, Michigan 49530

ISBN 978-0-310-28054-5

Interior design by Sherri Hoffman

Printed in the United States of America

13 14 • 21 20 19 18 17 16 15 14 13 12 11 10 9 8 7 6 5 4 3 2

CONTENTS

God has created us for community. This need is built into the very fiber of our being, the DNA of our spirit. As Christians, our deepest desire is to see the truth of God's Word as it influences our relationships with others. We long for a dynamic encounter with God's Word, intimate closeness with his people, and radical transformation of our lives. But how can we accomplish those three difficult tasks?

The New Community Bible Study Series creates a place for all of this to happen. In-depth Bible study, community-building opportunities, and life-changing applications are all built into every session of this small group study guide.

How to Build Community

How do we build a strong, healthy Christian community? The whole concept for this study grows out of a fundamental understanding of Christian community that is dynamic and transformational. We believe that Christians don't simply gather to exchange doctrinal affirmations. Rather, believers are called by God to get into each other's lives. We are family, for better or for worse, and we need to connect with each other.

Community is not built through sitting in the same building and singing the same songs. It is forged in the fires of life. When we know each other deeply—the good, the bad, and the ugly—community is experienced. Community grows when we learn to rejoice with one another, celebrating life. Roots grow deep when we know we are loved by others and are free to extend love to them as well. Finally, community deepens and is built when we commit to serve each other and let others serve us. This process of doing ministry and humbly receiving the ministry of others is critical for healthy community life.

Build Community Through Knowing and Being Known

We all long to know others deeply and to be fully known by them. Although we might run from this level of intimacy at times, we all want to have people in our lives who trust us enough to disclose the deep and tender parts of themselves. In turn, we want to reveal some of our feelings, expressing them freely to people we trust.

The first section of each of these six studies creates a place for deep knowing and being known. Through serious reflection on the truth of Scripture, you will be invited to communicate parts of your heart and life with your small group members. You might even discover yourself opening parts of your heart that you have thus far kept hidden. The Bible study and discussion questions do not encourage surface conversation. The only way to go deep in knowing others and being known by them is to dig deep, and this takes work. Knowing others also takes trust—that you will honor each other and respect each other's confidences.

Build Community Through Celebrating and Being Celebrated

If you have not had a good blush recently, read a short book in the Bible called Song of Songs. It's a record of a bride and groom writing poetic and romantic love letters to each other. They are freely celebrating every conceivable aspect of each other's personality, character, and physical appearance. At one point the groom says, "You have made my heart beat fast with a single glance from your eyes." Song of Songs is a reckless celebration of life, love, and all that is good.

We need to recapture the joy and freedom of celebration. In every session of this study, your group will commit to celebrate together. Although there are many ways to express joy, we will let our expression of celebration come through prayer. In each session you will take time to come before the God of joy and celebrate who he is and what he is doing. You will also have opportunity to celebrate what God is doing in your life and the lives of those who are a part of your small group. You will become a community of affirmation, celebration, and joy through your prayer time together.

You will need to be sensitive during this time of prayer together. Not everyone feels comfortable praying with a group of people. Be aware that each person is starting at a different place in their freedom to pray in a group, so be patient. Seek to promote a warm and welcoming atmosphere where each person can stretch a little and learn what it means to be a community that celebrates with God in the center.

Build Community Through Loving and Being Loved

Unless we are exchanging deeply committed levels of love with a few people, we will die slowly on the inside. This is precisely why so many people feel almost nothing at all. If we don't learn to exchange love with family and friends, we will eventually grow numb and no longer believe love is even a possibility. This is not God's plan. He hungers for us to be loved and to give love to others. As a matter of fact, he wants this for us even more than we want it for ourselves.

Every session in this study will address the area of loving and being loved. You will be challenged, in your personal life and as a small group, to be intentional and consistent about building loving relationships. You will get practical tools and be encouraged to set measurable goals for giving and receiving love.

Build Community Through Serving and Being Served

Community is about serving and humbly allowing others to serve you. The single most stirring example of this is recorded in John 13, where Jesus takes the position of the lowest servant and washes the feet of his followers. He gives them a powerful example and then calls them to follow. Servanthood is at the very core of community. To sustain deep relationships over a long period of time, there must be humility and a willingness to serve each other.

At the close of each session will be a clear challenge to servanthood. As a group, and as individual followers of Christ, you will discover that community is built through serving others. You will also find that your own small group members will grow in their ability to extend service to your life.

Bible Study Basics

To get the most out of this study, you will need to prepare and participate. Here are some guidelines to help you.

Preparing for the Study

1. If possible, even if you are not the leader, look over each session before you meet, read the Bible passages, and answer the questions. The more you are prepared, the more you will gain from the study.

2. Begin your preparation with prayer. Ask God to help you understand the passage and apply it to your life.

3. A good modern translation, such as the New International Version, Today's New International Version, the New American Standard Bible, or the New Revised Standard Version, will give you the most help. Questions in this guide are based on the New International Version.

4. Read and reread the passages. You must know what the passage says before you can understand what it means and how it applies to you.

5. Write your answers in the spaces provided in the study guide. This will help you participate more fully in the discussion and will also help you personalize what you are learning.

6. Keep a Bible dictionary handy to look up unfamiliar words, names, or places.

Participating in the Study

1. Be willing to join in the discussion. The leader of the group will not be lecturing but will encourage people to discuss what they have learned in the passage. Plan to share what God has taught you during your preparation time.

2. Stick to the passages being studied. Base your answers on the verses being discussed rather than on outside authorities such as commentaries or your favorite author or speaker.

HERE'S MY HEART LORD

3. Try to be sensitive to the other members of the group. Listen attentively when they speak, and be affirming whenever you can. This will encourage more hesistant members of the group to participate.
4. Be careful not to dominate the discussion. By all means participate, but allow others to have equal time.
5. If you are a discussion leader or a participant who wants further insights, you will find additional comments in the Leader's Notes at the back of the book.

2 Corinthians: Serving from the Heart

The founder of a business has a commitment to the organiza-tion because of the investment of blood, sweat, and tears it takes to get a company up and running. A mother has a spe-cial connection to a child because she carried that baby for nine months and then endured the process of giving birth ... she will never forget what it took to bring a baby into the world. When we study the second letter written to the church in the city of Corinth, we must understand that the apostle Paul planted this church (Acts 18). He had shared the gospel with many of these church members; he had helped them grow in faith; he had disciplined them when they were living in disobedience; he had cheered them on when they were heading in the right direction. Paul had a special place in his heart for the church in Corinth and for the Corinthian believers.

If you read the first letter to the Corinthian church you realize that Paul had already mentored and helped these people through some pretty serious issues and problems. Now, a group of false teachers (or false apostles) had arrived in Corinth and stirred up dissension and disunity in the church. This young congregation was facing attacks from outside and from inside.

Paul's second letter came as a challenge to keep the main thing the main thing. He did not want to see this gathering of Christ followers distracted from the mission God had placed before them. So he takes on these false teachers who he refers to as "super-apostles" (2 Corinthians 11:5). You can almost see the big "S" printed on their togas. They were making claims that Paul was not powerful enough, not eloquent enough, not stately enough to be a real apostle.

In response, Paul paints a beautiful picture of a Christlike life of service. He reminds the people that he came not to be a super-apostle but to suffer and serve like Jesus. Then he calls the people of Corinth to this same pathway of humble service.

In doing so, Paul is uncovering the sinister and ungodly spirit of the super-apostles.

It is sad to admit it but we need these same reminders in the church today. It seems the more things change, the more they remain the same. The culture of our time still lifts up the super-hero and forgets the humble servant.

Just think about how this message is reinforced in the movies with every new season of releases. Each year brings new examples. Certain names conjure vivid pictures in our minds: Sylvester Stallone, Chuck Norris, Arnold Schwarzenegger, Jean-Claude Van Damme, Harrison Ford, Brad Pitt, Tom Cruise, Jackie Chan, Matt Damon, and Will Smith are just some of the male examples. Pick up a DVD in which one of these stars headlines and you expect to see things blowing up, extended chase scenes, and scenes where the sweaty hero needs to have his shirt off while engaging in muscle-flexing activities. By the end of the movie, the bad guys are dead and the hero stands triumphant among the wreckage of his victory. This is the superhero genre in a nutshell.

I can vividly remember sitting in one of these action-packed movies with my wife Nancy at my side. At one point the hero character was between shirts . . . again. As the sun glistened off of his muscular bare chest I felt Nancy gently reach over and take my hand. She gave it a little squeeze and whispered something in my ear that I will never forget. She said to me, "You know, I am just not attracted to well-built men." I turned this comment over and over in my mind, searching for the compliment that I knew must be lurking somewhere beneath the surface, but it lurked so deep I never could find it.

If you don't believe people are drawn to movies that portray a victorious hero, just take a look at the top-selling movies of all time. In the top twenty-five grossing movies (as of 2008), a full eighteen of them follow the hero story line. Among them are five *Star Wars*, three *Lord of the Rings*, three *Spider-Mans*, and two *Pirates of the Caribbean*. Even the animated movies that become blockbusters (two *Shreks* and a *Lion King* are on that top twenty-five list) are about an overcoming hero. Very few of the movies in the top twenty-five are about the glory of being a servant. One exception is *The Passion of the Christ*.

Into our superhero-loving world comes a countercultural invitation: Be a servant. Let your heart be captured with a desire to humbly follow the way of Jesus. The second letter to the church at Corinth brings this message with clarity and passion. We are not called to be super-apostles or even super-Christians. We are called to the way of service, and this begins when our hearts align with the heart of Jesus. When that happens, the world will be transformed—not by force, domineering power, or flexed muscles, but as ordinary Christians extend the love, grace, and presence of Jesus with humble and authentic hearts.

BEGINNING WITH ROME, THE WAY WAS NEVER ACCOMPLISHED BY FORCE

Messengers of Reconciliation

2 CORINTHIANS 2:5–17; 5:14–21

From our first moments of life we are weighed, measured, and scored. It starts in the hospital minutes after our first breath. As our life goes on, we learn, almost by osmosis, that rewards follow good behavior. By the same token we come to understand that poor performance, in almost any area of life, will bring scowls rather than praise from peers, teachers, coaches, and sometimes even parents.

Trained rats run through a maze as fast as they can because they have learned they get a food pellet as a reward. Human beings play their own game of "rat-race." We perform, we strive, we work, we study, and at the end of each maze we push a little lever and out comes our reward pellet. It is just the way life works. "There is no free lunch." "You get what you deserve." "We pull ourselves up by our own bootstraps."

Then God comes into our cause-and-effect world and messes with the whole program. We believe people should get what they deserve, and Jesus dares to offer freely what we could never earn. The Bible is filled with reminders that the way of Jesus is radically countercultural:

> But God demonstrates his own love for us in this: While we were still sinners, Christ died for us. (Romans 5:8)

> For it is by grace you have been saved, through faith—and this not from yourselves, it is the gift of God—not by works, so that no one can boast. (Ephesians 2:8–9)

> This is how God showed his love among us: He sent his one and only Son into the world that we

might live through him. This is love: not that we loved God, but that he loved us and sent his Son as an atoning sacrifice for our sins. (1 John 4:9 – 10)

All those who want to be messengers of reconciliation must be ready to abandon the "cause-and-effect program" instituted by the world and taught to us from childhood. Instead, we need to freely embrace God's "grace program." When we do, we become Christ's ambassadors in a world filled with people who need the grace that God freely offers.

Making the Connection

1. How were you initiated into the "cause-and-effect program" that makes people feel like they only get what they earn and deserve in this life? *RAISED BY THE "GREATEST GENERATION"*

   How does God's "grace program" fly in the face of conventional wisdom that says we only get what we earn in this life? *Freely GIVEN SOMETHING THAT CAN NOT BE EARNED.*

Knowing and Being Known

Read 2 Corinthians 5:14 – 21

2. According to this passage, what is God's part in the ministry of reconciliation? *GOD RECONCILED US THRU JESUS*

3. God wants his people to be messengers of reconciliation. What does God want to do in us and through us to bring the message of reconciliation to the world? *IN Christ THE NEW IS HERE. THE OLD IS GONE. BE AMBASSADORS.*

Compelled by Love

I was not being nosy. I could not help but see the large picture of a little boy taking his first steps. The gentleman sitting next to me on the plane had fired up his computer and the screen saver popped up. I politely asked about the picture and this invited an avalanche of information, stories, and parental praise about his gifted and only child. I exhibited self-control and refrained from telling him that all of the amazing exploits of his son were actually quite common. The truth is, he loved his little boy and everything this little guy did brought joy to his daddy.

I am confident that when this loving father walked through the door of his home later that day, his son walked to him as fast as his wobbling young legs could carry him and embraced his daddy fiercely. We can all picture a little one moving toward their daddy or mommy with arms stretched upward. In that last step they do a lunge-fall into the embrace of a loving parent.

It is love that was compelling that father to hurry home to see his son. Love would move that little boy to throw himself into his father's arms. It is this same exchange of love with our heavenly Father that compels followers of Jesus to receive and pass on the message of reconciliation. It all starts with love. When we receive the amazing grace of God offered in Jesus, love overflows and moves us to raise our arms upward toward our heavenly Father and outward toward a world in need.

Read 2 Corinthians 5:14–15 and Isaiah 52:13–53:12

4. Jesus lived, suffered, died, and rose again for us. He willingly took the punishment we deserved for our sins. What images and messages of God's love come through these passages?

5. How have you experienced the love of God in your life and how does this compel you to do *one* of the following:
    • Respond back to God as a loving child
    • Live and walk in obedience to his purposes for your life
    • Be an ambassador of his love and grace to others

A New Creation

Flower markets and meat markets have one thing in common: a unique smell. Of course, it is not the same smell. If you have ever walked into a flower market you know the stunning aroma of hundreds of flowers. The fragrance is amazing, a mixture of scents that can be quite powerful. A meat market also has its own distinct aroma, a smell that is pungent and sometimes overwhelming. It does not take a trained nose to distinguish between a rose and a pork roast.

God wants us to know that followers of Christ have a fragrance for all the world to smell. Our scent is more powerful than bouquets of flowers or slabs of meat. We bear the fragrance of Christ wherever we go. Like a pine-scented car freshener dangling from the mirror, Jesus is in us and on us wherever we go. What is interesting is that various people we meet will "smell Jesus" in very different ways. To some the scent of Jesus on us will smell like life; to others it will smell like death.

Read 2 Corinthians 5:16 – 17 and 2:14 – 17

6. Every follower of Christ is a new creation who bears the aroma of Christ. Imagine a pollster was to ask your family, friends, neighbors, and colleagues, "How is (your name) a new creation because of Christ in their life?" (This could be new things that have come or old things that have gone away.) What kinds of answers do you think these people would give about you?

The Ministry of Reconciliation

When we think of reconciliation our minds often race to what we need to do or how we need to act to deserve restoration in a relationship that has been broken. Being reconciled to God, and showing others the way to a right relationship with their Maker, is not about what we do, but what God has done through Christ. Scott J. Hafemann writes:

"In our day of self-help and age of technology and technique, it is important to keep in mind that God is both the initiator and object of this reconciliation. Our propensity is to view the gospel as our opportunity to reconcile God to us by showing him how much we love him, rather than seeing it as God's act in Christ by which he reconciles us to himself by demonstrating his own love for us. The gospel is not our chance to get right with God, but God's declaration that he has already made us right with him. The gospel does not call us to do something for God that he might save us; it announces what God has done to save us that we might trust him." (*The NIV Application Commentary: 2 Corinthians*)

7. Those who know Jesus and who carry the fragrance of his presence into the world bear both the "smell of death" and the "fragrance of life." What does it mean to bear the "smell of death," and how have you seen this happen?

What does it mean to bear the "fragrance of life," and how have you seen this?

Read 2 Corinthians 5:18 – 19

8. What are some of the logical consequences and conclusions we will face if we believe that reconciliation to God comes because of how good we act or how much we prove our love for God?

What are some of the logical consequences and conclusions we will experience if we are confident that reconciliation comes because of what God has done in Jesus Christ, and that this is offered to us freely as a gift?

Ministers of Reconciliation

Most of us identify with the term *ambassador* primarily in a political context. This significant role normally places a person in a foreign land to represent their home country. An ambassador from the United States who lives and works in Japan is there to speak for America. When the Japanese people look at this ambassador, evaluate his actions, identify his motives, and investigate his lifestyle, it reflects substantially on how they view all Americans.

Christians are God's ambassadors in this world. It is as if God is speaking his words through each of his followers. What a staggering responsibility! What an honor! God has already done everything that needs to be done for lost and sinful people to be reconciled to him. Jesus, the sinless Lamb of God, has paid the price. As his ambassadors, we are called to invite people to accept this amazing work of reconciliation and be restored to a healed and whole relationship with God.

Read 2 Corinthians 5:20–21 and Ephesians 6:19–20

9. Each of us has relationships with people who have not yet received the reconciliation God offers through Jesus. Who are one or two of these people, and how has God connected your life with theirs?

10. The hard work of reconciliation has already been done by God. What are some specific and daily ways we can invite people to be reconciled to God?

11. How can your group members pray for you and encourage you as you seek to be God's ambassador right where he has placed you?

Celebrating and Being Celebrated

The introduction to this session (pages 15 – 16) includes three passages that remind us of the Father's love and the sacrifice of Jesus. Read these passages and also 2 Corinthians 5:21. Spend time offering prayers of praise and celebration in response to the amazing spiritual truths revealed in these portions of the Bible.

Loving and Being Loved

When we become new creations in Christ and live as ambassadors of reconciliation, this passion for reconciliation pours over into every relationship in our lives. Yes, God calls us to invite others to be reconciled to him. But he also teaches us to seek restoration with family members, in our friendships, and with anyone else with whom we may be at odds.

Take time this week to read 2 Corinthians 2:5 – 11. Once you have read the passage a couple of times, reflect on the questions below:

- Who needs to receive forgiveness from me?
- What steps can I take to extend forgiveness?
- Who needs to hear me reaffirm my love?
- What could I say or do to express love to this person?
- When we refuse to forgive and allow God to restore broken relationships, how does this play into the hands of Satan's schemes?

Serving and Being Served

One of the best ways we can serve the people God has placed in our lives is to help them discover the reconciling power of God's love and Jesus' grace. Make a list of people you know who need to experience the reconciling power of God. On your list, place their name, relationship to you, and specific prayer needs you know they have at this time in their life:

Name: Relationship: Specific Prayers:

1.

2.

3.

4.

5.

Commit to pray in the following ways for these people during the weeks you are part of this small group study:

- Pray for the needs each person is experiencing in their life.
- Pray for each heart to be soft and receptive to whatever God wants to do.
- Ask for God to use you as an ambassador of his message of reconciliation to each of these people.
- Invite the Holy Spirit to give you boldness to find some way to let each of these people know that they can be reconciled to God.

The Power of Endurance

2 CORINTHIANS 1:3–7; 4:7–18; 6:3–10; 11:16–29

In the early part of the twentieth century lived a concert pianist named Ignacy Jan Paderewski (1860–1941). There is a story told of him, true as far as I know, about a time he was giving a concert in a great auditorium. All the people were gathered and waiting. Paderewski was delayed in coming out to the stage and the crowd was slowly growing restless. A nine-year-old boy, who had been dragged to the concert by his mother, became particularly bored. No one seemed to notice the inconspicuous child as he got up, walked down the aisle, and began to ascend the stairs. There was a hush followed by a growing murmur as he sat down at the piano and started to play "Chopsticks." It was the only song he knew.

All of a sudden the people in the auditorium were buzzing. "Get that kid out of there. What is he doing?" Any mother could imagine what went through the mind and heart of the boy's mom as she realized that the child at the piano was her son.

From the wings of the stage Paderewski heard what was happening. Instead of calling for an usher to remove the boy he simply put on his tuxedo jacket, walked over to the piano, reached his two big arms on either side of this little boy, and began to play an improvised accompaniment. Paderewski leaned toward the boy and whispered, "Don't quit. Just keep playing. You are doing great. Don't stop. Don't stop." And what started out as a bit ordinary became a masterpiece together.

God wants every one of his children to know there is a deeper music to their life than they could possibly dream. As we go about our daily lives, do the simple things, and play our personal version of "Chopsticks," God cheers us on. He puts his arms around us, adds his presence, power, and music, and says, "Don't quit, hang in there, endure, and just watch what we can do together." God invites us to endure in the ordinary stuff of life — doing our work well, getting an education, raising children, building a strong marriage, caring for our body, growing friendships, and a thousand things that can seem mundane at times. He also calls us to walk in the power of endurance when we face deep loss, relational brokenness, financial challenges, relentless temptation, physical weariness, emotional turmoil, and a host of other struggles.

In the moments of life when we feel alone, weak, discouraged, outmatched, outwitted, tired, and ready to throw in the towel, we hear God's voice whisper in our ear. He says, "Keep playing. Don't stop. Hang in there. Endure." Then, when we listen closely, we realize that our song might be simple and seem ordinary, but God is playing also. He adds what we lack, and it is beautiful ... a masterpiece. The power to endure is not something we just dig out of our own resources and abilities. It comes when we realize we're at the end of ourselves and must learn to rely on the One who can provide abundantly more than we will ever need.

Making the Connection

1. Tell about a time you felt like quitting and throwing in the towel, but you endured and hung in there with God's help. As you look back, why are you glad you endured?

    We all have started things only to give up along the way. Tell about one such experience that you look back on and say, "I wish I had hung in there and endured."

26

Knowing and Being Known

Read 2 Corinthians 6:3–10 and 11:16–29

2. What were some of the things the apostle Paul had to endure as he followed God's plan for his life?

3. How do you think Paul might respond to this statement: "If Christians follow God's will and walk in true faith, they will experience only health, wealth, and peace-filled days"?

Paul's Experience of Endurance

Far from seeing his weakness and suffering as evidence *against* his ministry, Paul says that they are in fact *proof* of his ministry. Paul had learned that however great the problem or challenge, it could never pry him away from Christ's grip on him and his grip on Christ. He held fast to the faith. He didn't quit. Through it all, Paul endured by God's grace and power. Through his sufferings Paul entered a whole new realm of spiritual life and trust in God. He learned that God is at work in and through our sufferings in ways we cannot see and may not understand.

Paul uses a Greek word that is translated "hardship" and was used to describe situations that seem overwhelming or insurmountable. When we read Paul's story of walking with Jesus, it feels like he went from one overwhelming challenge to the next. Yet he always had a sense that God was with him and he would make it through. When he faced these intense times of struggle and endurance, Paul saw them as part of his journey of faith. They drew him closer to God. Paul did not identify hardships, struggles, times of distress, or persecutions as signs of faithlessness but as opportunities to grow more faithful, more like the One who suffered for him ... Jesus.

Read Romans 5:1 – 5 and 2 Corinthians 6:3 – 10

4. Imagine you had a chance to interview Paul near the end of his life. How do you think he might respond to the following questions?

    • What are some of the benefits of facing hard times and enduring through them?

    • What advice would you give to persons who spend a great deal of time and energy trying to set up a life where they never struggle or suffer?

    • If you could go back and behave differently so that you could avoid some of the severe physical, emotional, and relational pain you have endured, what would you change?

    • What would you tell parents who are committed to work as hard as they can to "protect" their children from pain and struggle?

    • How has facing hardships and suffering drawn you closer to Jesus and made you more like Jesus?

5. We all face times of struggle and hardship in this life. What can drive a person to throw in the towel and give up rather than endure through difficult times?

6. What are some practical actions you find help you endure and stand strong when life is filled with struggles and hardships?

Enduring through "Light" and "Momentary" Troubles

Paul reflects on what he and his colleagues in ministry have faced and uses terms like, "hard pressed ... perplexed ... persecuted ... and struck down." He even talks about being "given over to death." Paul is speaking about intense suffering, but he seems to have this resilient sense of hope and strength that helps him endure. He has a perspective that makes the reader wonder, "Does this guy really see what he is facing and how hard he has it?" We wonder, *How can someone who has gone through what Paul has experienced keep pressing on?* But then he pulls back the veil and shows why he can remain strong, hopeful, and sane in the midst of indescribable life-struggles. He writes:

Therefore we do not lose heart. Though outwardly we are wasting away, yet inwardly we are being renewed day by day. For our light and momentary troubles are achieving for us an eternal glory that far outweighs them all. So we fix our eyes not on what is seen, but on what is unseen. For what is seen is temporary, but what is unseen is eternal. (2 Corinthians 4:16–18)

Paul is talking about intense suffering, beatings, spiritual battles, imprisonment, hunger, rejection, sleeplessness, affliction, and the two adjectives he uses to describe this suffering are "light" and "momentary." Wow! How can Paul have this kind of perspective?

The only way the apostle Paul can see things this way, and the only way we can live with a confident sense that our struggles and sufferings are light and momentary, is if we adopt a kingdom mind-set. We make this shift when we see this life and what we experience as only part of the story. When our perspective changes, our attitude follows.

Paul is not being glib. He is not minimizing human suffering. *Light* is a comparative term. If you are going to call something light, it depends on what you are comparing it to. Paul says in essence, "Put human suffering on one side of the scale, and then put the weight of the glory that is destined for us on the other side of the scale, and suffering does not even register. It is no contest." *Momentary* is also a comparative term. The glory God has for us is eternal in nature and our suffering is only for this life. It is here and then it will be gone, like a morning mist that melts away as the sun rises. Compared to the infinite weight of glory and eternal hope we have in Jesus, any hardship we face in this life really is light and momentary.

Read 2 Corinthians 4:7–18

7. Paul teaches that one way we keep our perspective right is to fix our eyes on what is "unseen" and "eternal." When troubles come, and they will come, what are some of the "eternal" and "unseen" things we can fix our eyes on that will keep our perspective right?

8. God takes our pain and suffering in this life very seriously. He offers comfort through the Holy Spirit and calls followers of Jesus to care for and minister to each other. The Psalms are filled with honest prayers of lament, struggle, and heartache. These portions of Scripture reassure us that faithful Christians can express sorrow and struggle. How is each of the following statements true?

- The suffering and struggles of this life are "light" and "momentary," and we should not be consumed or paralyzed by them . . . we can endure and press on!

- Our struggles and heartache in this life are real and they matter to God . . . we should not take them lightly but look to God for comfort and strength.

9. Second Corinthians 4:7 – 18 is filled with contrasts. Here are some of them:

We are:	We are not:
Hard pressed	Crushed
Perplexed	In despair
Persecuted	Abandoned
Struck down	Destroyed
Outwardly wasting away	Losing heart

Describe how you have experienced one of these contrasting realities as you live for Jesus in a world filled with struggles and suffering.

Fruit of Endurance

Endurance is not about hanging in there until we die or Jesus returns. There is so much more to it. When we learn to endure and stand strong as we face pain and sorrow in this life, God refines, purifies, and grows us in the process. We become more like Jesus and are prepared to live for him and serve others with greater passion.

When we walk through the fires of this life, Jesus walks with us. When we are broken, God shows up and heals us. When we are hurting, the Holy Spirit of God comes as the great Comforter and cares for us. We meet God in the furnaces of life and come out stronger. Then, to our surprise, the very struggle we faced becomes an opportunity to minister to a person who is facing similar pain and hurt.

Read 2 Corinthians 1:3 – 7

10. Tell about a time God used someone who had gone through sorrow and suffering to minister to you when you faced a similar situation.

How did their experience of God's comfort and care become a tool for the Holy Spirit to minister through them to you?

11. What furnace or experience of suffering have you faced, and how might God use you to bring comfort and encouragement to someone who will face this same pain in their future?

Celebrating and Being Celebrated

Read 2 Corinthians 1:3–7 as a group, then pray as follows:
- Thank God for the people he has sent into your life to minister comfort and compassion when you have gone through times of suffering and sorrow.
- Ask God to prepare you to minister to people who are going through pain and struggles in life. Invite the Holy Spirit to teach you endurance so that you will be ready to walk with others when they face the same hardships you have navigated with God's help and power.

Loving and Being Loved

In our times of deep sorrow, loss, and struggle, God often sends someone to walk by our side. As the apostle Paul puts it, there are people who offer us the very same comfort they received from God in their time of need. But when we are hurting we are often not at a place to express our appreciation for the very people who care for us the most. As a matter of fact, because we are facing personal pain and anguish, we can sometimes treat people harshly and unkindly as they seek to minister God's grace to us.

Take time this week to reflect on the last time you went through a furnace experience of struggle and pain. Who did God bring to your side? It could be a family member, friend, person from church, or anyone who became a vehicle for God's grace in your life. Now that you are past this time of struggle, be sure to thank this person for their care, ministry, and the comfort of the Holy Spirit they extended. Let them know how God worked through them. Share how your faith is deeper and your life is stronger because of their ministry to you.

Serving and Being Served

When we face hardships and pain in this life, it is important to remember two distinct things. First, God offers us power to endure through these "light" and "momentary" struggles. We can make it through and these things (no matter how big they feel) will look small in the rearview mirror of eternity. Second, God really cares about the losses and pain we face in this life. He wants to offer comfort and care through the power of his Holy Spirit. One of the ways God does this is through the way we care for each other and offer support in times of struggle.

If any of your group members is facing a time of hardship, talk about it together. Identify ways your group can offer prayer, support, and encouragement that will help this person endure and press on through this challenging time.

Pure Life

2 CORINTHIANS 6:14–7:1

Purity is a wonderful thing. When something is pure it exists in its essential nature: it is undefiled, unblemished, and uncontaminated. Purity is so important that a whole section of the U.S. federal government, the Food and Drug Administration (FDA), exists to monitor and protect the purity of our food supply. The idea of such a monitoring agency ought to bring us a great sense of comfort and security. But don't rejoice too quickly. The standards of purity held up by the federal government of the United States may surprise you. Here are a few examples:

Apple Butter—If the mold count in apple butter is 12 percent or more it gets recalled, but up to 12 percent is okay. If there is an average of four rodent hairs found in 100 grams or more, or an average of five or more whole insects, not counting mites, aphids, or scale insects (which apparently are not a problem), the apple butter can't be sold. But if there is a 11 percent mold count, three rodent hairs, four whole insects, and lots of mites and aphids, it is pure enough for you to spread on your toast in the morning.

Coffee Beans—If you are a passionate coffee drinker you might want to skip this part. If an average of 10 percent or more of the coffee beans in a container are insect infested, or if there is one live insect in each of two or more immediate containers, then it gets recalled. The FDA says people just don't like getting live insects with their coffee beans. But if only 9 percent of the beans are insect infested, that batch is pure enough for sale and consumption. I'll have a grande, nonfat, triple-shot Bugaccino.

Mushrooms—If there is an average of twenty or more maggots of any size per fifteen grams of dry mushrooms, they are declared unsuitable. But nineteen maggots, big or small, are the standard of purity.

Fig Paste and Hot Dogs—You do not want to know.

The point is that the standard for purity is not nearly as high as we might expect or hope. Now imagine for a moment that the scope of the FDA was expanded and it became the FDCA: the Food, Drug, and Character Association. What if the government tried to set standards for purity of the human heart? What might these standards look like?

Making the Connection

1. Our culture uses a sliding scale not only for the purity of food and but also for moral purity. How might a cultural definition of purity differ from God's standard for moral purity in *some* of the following areas:

   - What it means to speak pure words
   - How we use our eyes to look at people
   - How we deal with anger, revenge, and judging people
   - Sexual purity for those who are married
   - Sexual purity for those who are single
   - Purity in our thought lives
   - The kinds of images and pictures we view on TV, computer, and movie screens

Welcome to Corinth

We've all seen signs as we've entered cities or crossed state lines that give a welcome and announce themselves as, "The Friendliest City Around," "The Sunshine State," or "A Growing Community with a Small-Town Feel." If there had been a sign welcoming people to ancient Corinth it might have read, "Welcome to Sin City!" Their motto could have been, "What happens in Corinth stays in Corinth!"

Because of its strategic location, the city was often called "Wealthy Corinth." Ancient writers referred to this city as the "epitome of crass materialism." One first-century author wrote, "Corinth is filled with crowds of wretched demagogues around the temples shouting and abusing one another. Corinth is filled with fortune-tellers trying to exploit people for money. Corinth is filled with hucksters peddling whatever they could lay their hands on. Corinth is filled with innumerable lawyers perverting justice."

Corinth was also home to temples for at least four Greek gods, a center of Roman emperor worship, and the site for worship of Egyptian gods who were imported by Egyptian sailors. All of these different cults, temples, and pagan forms of worship coexisted in pluralistic Corinth, and most citizens saw no problem worshiping a multitude of gods. The main shrine in Corinth was the temple of Aphrodite, the Greek goddess of love. One scholar wrote that this temple was so rich that it boasted a thousand temple prostitutes. There was a direct correlation between idol worship and sexual immorality—the two went hand in hand.

The term to *Corinthianize* actually became a euphemism in Paul's day for immorality in general, and sexual immorality in particular. When people talked about someone who was steeped in sexual immorality, they would talk about somebody Corinthianizing. Just try to picture a society that is crude, pluralistic, materialistic, sexually obsessed, and superficial—and it is all seen as normal behavior. Does this sound vaguely familiar? Does it describe any modern culture you might have heard of?

Read 2 Corinthians 6:14 – 7:1

2. What are some of the warnings found in this passage, and how can heeding them help a follower of Christ grow in purity?

3. With what you know of the city of Corinth (think of the struggles and sins addressed in 1 – 2 Corinthians), how is our culture today similar to ancient Corinth?

Walking Closely with the Father

Paul says, "Since we have these promises, let us purify ourselves." The primary promise he is talking about is that God will be with his children. Like a loving father he will watch over us, walk with us, and hold our hand as we travel through a world filled with sinful practices and perpetual temptation. There is a possessiveness that God has for his people. "I will be your Father, and you shall be my sons and daughters." Knowing this will help us seek to purify ourselves from everything that could contaminate our body and spirit. God offers his powerful presence voluntarily, no strings attached; we don't have to earn it.

Nothing will help followers of Jesus seek purity with greater passion than a profound awareness that our heavenly Father is with us. Imagine each of these Christian people walking into a real-life situation with a vivid picture of God holding their hand and walking right at their side: a business person away for a couple of days in a town that promises total anonymity; a student living on a university campus for the very first time; a church leader sitting in his or her office doing an Internet search; a couple preparing their taxes; a single person out on a date. When we know we are living and walking in the very presence of our loving Father, both the desire and strength to live purely increases.

Read 2 Corinthians 6:16, 18 and 7:1

4. How does a deep and profound awareness of God's presence help do the following:

- Increase awareness that temptation and sin are present

- Reduce our desire to sin and make impure decisions

- Grant strength to say no to temptations and the entice-ments of sin

- Create a desire to purify ourselves from the things that can contaminate our body and spirit

5. What helps you grow in your awareness of God's presence with you in all of life's circumstances?

What are some of the things that tend to block out our awareness of God's presence as we walk through the day, and how can we remove these obstacles?

Don't Be Unequally Yoked ... The Issue of Who

The term "being yoked" made sense to people in the first century, but today many of us have no idea what it means. The picture is really quite simple and profound. A yoke was the instrument that was placed over the shoulders of two animals so they could walk side by side and pull a plow or cart together. When the animals were evenly yoked the work went well; when they weren't, the work was painful and unproductive. To be evenly yoked usually meant they were of similar size, had a stride that matched the other animal, and would pull in the same direction. A smart farmer would never yoke together two animals that would work against each other.

When Paul says, "Do not be yoked together with unbelievers," he is not talking about a casual acquaintance. He is not saying, "Have nothing to do with unbelievers." As a matter of fact, all through the Bible followers of Christ are called to connect with, befriend, and love those who are far from God. So what is Paul getting at? He is using the image of a yoke to point out a special kind of relationship, the kind that will significantly impact the trajectory of one's life. Paul is saying, "There are going to be certain key relationships in your life that will set the direction of all you do and who you will become. In these relationships, be very careful. Make sure you are yoked to people who have similar faith, values, life-vision, stride, and direction." Do you start to get the picture of two people walking as they are yoked together? If you are yoked to someone who is consistently walking in a different direction ... ouch!

Read 2 Corinthians 6:14 – 16 and 1 Corinthians 15:33 – 34

6. What are some possible benefits and strengths of being yoked to another committed follower of Christ in *one* of the following areas of life?
   - In a business partnership
   - In a marriage relationship
   - In a very close and confidential friendship
   - In a mentoring or coaching relationship

How can you increase and develop more of these kinds of "evenly yoked" relationships?

7. What are some possible consequences or struggles that could surface if you are yoked to a person who is not a committed follower of Jesus in *one* of these same relationships?
   - In a business partnership
   - In a marriage relationship
   - In a very close and confidential friendship
   - In a mentoring or coaching relationship

What counsel would you give to a follower of Jesus who is considering being yoked to a nonbeliever in one of these areas?

Touch Nothing Unclean ... The Issue of What

We grow in purity as we walk closely, hand in hand, with our loving Father. We strengthen our purity quotient when we are sensitive to the "who" of life ... who should I be closely yoked with? In addition, there is a "what" factor to our growth in purity. We need to begin asking, "What should I touch and what should I refrain from touching?" Quoting from the Old Testament, Paul exhorts us: "Touch no unclean thing." In those days a whole list of things were declared "unclean." People knew the list and avoided touching those things. For us today, it is a little more complicated.

An unclean thing is whatever keeps us from walking closely with God. It could be almost anything. We must be prayerful, wise, and humble as we seek to identify these "unclean things," then make a decision to eliminate them. It might be the remote control or a credit card. For some it is less tangible, like avoiding selfish ambition. It could be a relationship that is headed in an unhealthy direction, a problem with anger, or a character issue. The best person to identify what will push you from God and wander from purity is you. It is also helpful to listen to the counsel of Christian friends and family members who know us and love us.

Read 2 Corinthians 6:17

8. Take a moment to list some of the "unclean things" you think people in our culture should stop "touching" or "pursuing."

Why are these things so prevalent, and how do they lead to an impure culture?

9. "Clean things" are whatever draw you closer to God; "unclean things" are what drive you away from him. Identify some of the "clean" and "unclean" things in your own life:

Clean Things (Draw me close to God):	Unclean Things (Push me away from God):

How can you be more intentional about taking hold of "clean things" that will help you grow in purity?

What can you do to keep from touching "unclean things" and avoid impurity?

Come Out and Be Separate ... The Issue of Where

When we live in a place like Corinth long enough, we can get used to it. It is like the proverbial frog in the kettle: the temperature gradually keeps rising, but the frog doesn't even notice. Similarly, when we see impurity often enough, it stops bothering us to the point that we don't even notice it anymore.

With this human tendency in mind, Paul says, "Come out from them and be separate." This does not mean we have to run away from Corinth. The truth is, we can't escape being in this world and we should not try to. But we do have to stay attentive, becoming keenly aware of the places impurity exists and grows. In that way, we can avoid the specific circumstances and situations in which we could be lured into sinful practices that lead to impurity. It *is* possible to live in the world and not be molded into its image. By keeping our eyes open, we can walk through a world that celebrates impurity and still live as the dwelling place of a holy God.

Read 2 Corinthians 6:17 and Romans 12:1 – 2

10. If we are not careful, living in this world will numb us to the presence and power of impurity. What are some things that most Christ followers and the church used to see as impure, but now these actions, attitudes, or practices are slowly becoming accepted?

What can we do to step back from the influence of the world and get a fresh and godly perspective?

11. We can't leave this world, but we can choose to avoid some places. Name some places you find it is best to avoid because of the enticement to sin and impurity.

Celebrating and Being Celebrated

In a world of impurity, followers of Christ are still called to live and grow in holiness. As a matter of fact, God calls us to something extraordinary. He says,

> "I am the LORD your God; consecrate yourselves and be holy, because I am holy. Do not make yourselves unclean by any creature that moves about on the ground. I am the LORD who brought you up out of Egypt to be your God; therefore be holy, because I am holy" (Leviticus 11:44–45).

Just think about that for a moment. The standard of holiness and purity for our lives is the character and holiness of God. This high calling is not meant to discourage us, but to give us a goal, a vision, a dream for deeper levels of purity than we ever imagined.

Take time as a group to pray in three distinct directions:
- Worship God for his purity and celebrate his holiness.
- Thank Jesus for the holiness he bestows on us because he cleansed us from sin through his death on the cross.
- Ask the Holy Spirit to give you wisdom and power to walk closely with the Father, to avoid being unevenly yoked, to keep from touching unclean things, and to know when to be separate from the world.

Loving and Being Loved

The world is filled with impurity and sin. But God still loves the world and so should we. As his follower and an ambassador of his grace in this world, commit to pray for the world. Take time in the coming week to pray for some of the following:

- For leaders in your local, state, and national government
- For believers to stay *in* the world, even the tough places, but not be *of* the world
- For God's love to flow through you as you walk daily wherever God sends you
- For revival and renewal to cover the face of the earth
- For Christians to take a role of godly and humble leadership in every level of society

Serving and Being Served

Too often Christians withdraw from arenas where we could have an influence and bring the presence of Jesus. Though there are times we need to step back, we also need to learn to step forward. Christians should be first in line to serve in all sorts of settings. Take time to evaluate your life and schedule to see if you are making space to serve in your community. You might coach a kids' sports team, volunteer at school as a tutor, serve meals at a shelter, be on a city board, or find another way to contribute. As you serve, pray for the grace and presence of Jesus to be felt by those you encounter.

Gracious Generosity

2 CORINTHIANS 8:1–12

If you have a wallet or purse, take it out and hold it in your hands. Really ... while this is being read, hold this item in front of you where you can see it. Think about what this object represents: the place people keep their cash, credit cards, and checks. What you hold in your hands can become a modern-day temple.

Whenever we talk about money, deep issues of trust begin to surface. For many people, the primary place they put their trust is in their financial worth. If they have enough money and stuff, they feel secure. If they are lacking in the cash department, they feel worried and unstable. Some people live as if the content of their checking or savings account defines their ability to experience happiness.

It is important to note that the Bible does not say money is bad or evil. But it does give warnings about falling in love with money and the stuff of this world.

> People who want to get rich fall into temptation and a trap and into many foolish and harmful desires that plunge men into ruin and destruction. For the love of money is a root of all kinds of evil. Some people, eager for money, have wandered from the faith and pierced themselves with many griefs. (1 Timothy 6:9–10)

> No one can serve two masters. Either he will hate the one and love the other, or he will be devoted to the one and despise the other. You cannot serve both God and Money. (Matthew 6:24)

Keep your lives free from the love of money and be content with what you have, because God has said, "Never will I leave you; never will I forsake you." (Hebrews 13:5)

The truth is, as fallen creatures, we are tempted to give money and possessions the power to make us feel secure, successful, valuable, the source of our hope and peace. Or, we can let them make us feel weak, worthless, and insignificant. But God wants us to learn a different reality. Rather than clutch our wallet or purse to our chest and protect what we have, he invites us to lift it up and offer it to him. Only then will we experience the joy and freedom of living with gracious generosity.

Making the Connection

1. How does our culture encourage a lifestyle where money becomes an idol and a source of security?

Knowing and Being Known

Read 2 Corinthians 8:1 – 15 and 9:6 – 15

2. The churches in Macedonia had learned the secret of joyful generosity. Describe the hearts of the Christians in Macedonia when it came to how they viewed giving and helping others.

Describe the actions of the Macedonian Christians and how their behavior might have been seen as unusual back then and even today.

3. These passages contain many insights about what gracious generosity can look like. What is the right attitude and spirit for giving?

What are some results when we give with gracious generosity?

What is the connection between a willing spirit and giving?

Strange Math

We all think that if we just had more stuff we would be happier. But economist Richard Easterlin conducted research that proved that affluent people are no happier on average than nonaffluent people (provided basic needs are met). He found that an increase in wealth does *not* bring an increase in perceived happiness.

In a world where the accumulation of material goods is a pathological obsession, this revelation might come as a surprise. But it would not have shocked the Macedonian Christians. They had learned an equation that was just as strange in their day as it is in ours:

Abundant Joy + Extreme Poverty = A Wealth of Generosity

This might see counterintuitive. But it is true. The Macedonian believers were poor, but joyous. Out of this condition of the heart, generosity naturally overflowed. I also want to suggest that the reverse equation is also true:

Discontent + Extreme Affluence = A Famine of Generosity

The simple truth is that people don't start giving when they have more money, but when they have more joy. When joy invades our hearts we are no longer dependent on the contents of the wallet god or purse god to make us happy. When joy grows, generosity flows!

Read 2 Corinthians 8:1 – 2

4. Give an example or tell a story of how you have seen the Abundant Joy + Extreme Poverty = A Wealth of Generosity equation at work.

5. Give an example or tell a story of how you have seen the Discontent + Extreme Affluence = A Famine of Generosity equation at work.

Welcome to the Adventure

We live in a day and age where people spend huge amounts of money to experience unique adventures. From photo safaris in Africa to skiing the Alps to hiking the outback of Australia, people are becoming adventure junkies. God offers us an adventure more challenging and exciting than the wildest whitewater rafting trip; it's called extreme giving. This was the journey that the Macedonian Christians were on and it led to staggering levels of joy, adventure, and meaning.

Let your mind wrap around the experience of these first-century followers of Christ. Remember, these people were going through a time of severe trial and struggle, living in "extreme poverty." (Just for the record, extreme poverty in the first century was far worse than most of us can imagine.) Out of this setting they began to climb upward on an adventure of giving that involved four peaks ... each one higher than the one before.

First, they began to *give with rich generosity.* Second, they *gave as much as they were able* ... they pushed themselves upward in giving. Third, they *gave beyond their ability.* Then, the final, Mount Everest peak on the adventure of giving ... they *pleaded (with urgency) to have the privilege of continuing in the ministry of giving* and helping others who were poor. This could be called "the adventure of extreme giving." It is a journey that every Christ follower should consider taking.

Read 2 Corinthians 8:3 – 7 and 9:11 – 15

6. What needs are people trying to meet when they take adventure trips or try new and potentially dangerous things?

How could entering into extreme giving fulfill the desire for adventure in this life?

What are some of the risks and rewards of extreme giving?

7. Look at the mountain peaks and categories below and identify where you see yourself on this adventure (start at the
bottom of the mountain with Stage 0):

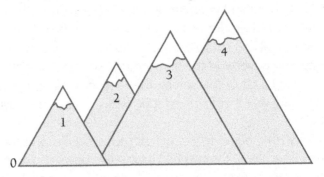

Stage 0. I have not started the journey.
Stage 1. I am learning to give and become generous.
Stage 2. I am learning to give as much as I am able
(stretching myself as I give).
Stage 3. I am learning to give beyond my ability.
Stage 4. I am pleading with God and looking for oppor-
tunities to give more.

*What keeps you from taking the next step on this adventure of
giving?*

What could you do to take the next step?

God, Grace, and Giving

There is this intimate connection in Paul's mind between giving and grace. Authentic, generous, freely offered giving is an unmistakable sign of God's grace. Often, when we talk about grace, we restrict the discussion to the forgiveness of sins. But the grace of God is much more than his willingness to forgive sin. God was gracious before the fall ever occurred, before any sins needed to be forgiven. The word that lies at the heart of the grace of God is "give." To say that God is gracious is to say he is an irrepressible giver.

Paul is saying, "The same kind of grace that characterizes the heart of God should mark the lives of his people." That is why Paul is so careful to connect giving with grace and *not* the law. He is teaching that giving should flow from an awareness of God's grace and an organic desire to extend this gracious generosity to others. Giving is not to be forced or coerced, but should be the free expression of a generous heart. When the God of grace holds our heart, he also has our wallet or purse ... and giving becomes a natural response.

8. The concept of grace comes up six times in 2 Corinthians 8:1–9 and 9:6–15. What is the connection between grace and generosity?

9. As you have grown deeper in your awareness and experience of grace, how has it impacted the way you serve through the ministry of giving?

The Greatest Example

In our society the heroes with a story worth telling seem to be people who start poor and end up rich. This theme, the classic "rags to riches" formula, can be found in countless books and movies. Something in the fabric of the human heart is drawn to a character that works hard, climbs the ladder of life, and ends up on top.

But there is another world, another story, another kingdom. It is called the kingdom of God, and it is characterized by downward mobility. In this upside-down world the hero, Jesus Christ, starts out rich and becomes poor. He possessed all the riches of heaven, the splendor of glory, the worship of angels, and power beyond imagination. Yet he voluntarily left it all to be born in a filthy manger and raised in a blue-collar family, where he scraped out a living in an obscure village, became an itinerate teacher, and then died on a Roman cross. The story of Jesus is not a celebration of poverty. Rather, it is a picture of radical giving and service, an example of what it looks like to reverse the story and choose the pathway of humble service and generous giving.

Read 2 Corinthians 8:9 and Philippians 2:5 – 8

10. What are some of the ways the life of Jesus is a story of "riches to rags" rather than "rags to riches"?

11. How can we consciously choose to follow the example of Jesus and serve others through a commitment to give generously?

Celebrating and Being Celebrated

All through the Bible we are taught that every good gift we have is from the hand of God (see, for example, James 1:17). Take a few moments to list some of the good gifts you have from God. Then, as a group, pray as follows:

- First, thank God for his goodness and generosity toward you. Lift up specific thanks for his provision of good gifts.
- Second, ask for a heart so filled with grace that you increase in your desire to share what you have with others. Pray for a heart like Jesus that is ready to pour out what you have for the sake of blessing others.

Loving and Being Loved

As we receive God's grace and become more like Jesus, our generosity grows. As we express this generosity in practical ways, we find ourselves serving those in the church and outside of the church through what we give. We should all receive the challenge that comes through the example of the Macedonian Christians, through the teaching of the apostle Paul, and through the life of Jesus. As we do, we will make choices that lead toward gracious generosity.

What challenge do you need to take as you enter the quest to excel in the grace of giving? It will look different for each follower of Christ. Some have not yet started a discipline of giving and the first step is to start giving something ... get in the game ... start somewhere. It is not about pressure or compulsion but a natural response to the grace of God. Others might have been giving inconsistently and the next step is developing a regular discipline of giving with a joyful, generous heart. Some people might be giving a full tithe (10 percent) but they feel the call to increase their percentage even higher, in order to excel in the grace of giving. No matter where you are on the journey, focus on the grace of God, pray for courage to press forward on the adventure, and take another step of growth in generosity.

Serving and Being Served

Sometime this week, when you make time for prayer, pull out your wallet, checkbook, or purse. Set it on your lap and think about what this object represents. For many people it has become an idol. Money has ruled their life. As you think about what this item represents, say to God, "It's all yours. It all belongs to you. I will hold the things of the world loosely and I will hold your hand tightly. Please help me to be so overwhelmed by your grace that generosity will flow freely from me. Make me more like Jesus, who gave away everything and became poor so that I might inherit the riches of heaven."

The Right Motivation for Serving

2 CORINTHIANS 10:1–18

A serious addiction problem affects many people rich and poor, young and old, of every race and creed. This particular addiction has nothing to do with chemical dependency or substance abuse. To date, there are no Twelve-Step groups or treatment centers to help people fight it. Many who are afflicted with this sickness do not even know it.

It is called "approval addiction": living in bondage to what other people think. If your identity is wrapped up in whether or not you are perceived as successful, likable, or acceptable, you are predisposed to become an approval addict. When you become an approval addict, no matter how much of this drug you get, you can never have enough. Just like all other junkies, you need more and more.

Henri Nouwen puts it like this, "Who am I? I am the one who is liked, praised, admired, disliked, hated or despised." In other words, when you are in the grips of approval addiction, you are what people think of you. Whether you are a pianist, businessperson, teacher, homemaker, minister, or a newspaper reporter, what matters, what drives you, is how you're perceived by others. This is the life of an approval addict.

If being busy is important, then I must be busy. If having money is a sign of real freedom, then I must increase my net worth, or at least make people think I have increased it. If knowing many people proves my importance, I will make the necessary contacts and build the relational bridges that will make me look good. What matters is how I am perceived by my world.

Because approval addicts are always vulnerable to other people's opinions, life becomes an emotional roller coaster ... and it seems the lows are always more profound than the highs.

Making the Connection

1. As you read the following symptoms of approval addiction (a partial list), place a mental check in each box that applies to you:

   ☐ I'm easily hurt by things other people say about me.
   ☐ I often compare myself to other people, even people I don't know very well.
   ☐ I'm very competitive and have an unexplainable need to beat other people and be number one.
   ☐ I live with a nagging sense that I am not all that important or special and I am jealous of those who seem to be "important" to others.
   ☐ I try to impress others by subtly boasting about myself.
   ☐ I avoid confronting people because I am afraid they won't like me if I do.
   ☐ I find myself wondering, "What do other people think about me?"

   The truth is, almost every human being who walks the earth has moments when this virus of the soul attacks. Why is approval addiction so common and prevalent?

   What is one way you have seen a symptom of approval addiction show up in your life?

Knowing and Being Known

Read 2 Corinthians 10:1 – 18

2. There was obviously some kind of debate among the Christians in Corinth about the apostle Paul, centering on why he seemed "timid and unimpressive" sometimes but "bold and forceful" at others. What was the substance of this debate?

How do you think Paul would explain or reconcile these two seemingly contradictory aspects of his personality?

The Approval of God ... Our Source of Freedom

The Corinthians were confused because sometimes Paul seemed so gentle and other times so powerful. Would the real Paul please stand up? They had never met someone who was so free from approval addiction, so unconcerned with what others thought. Because Paul's focus and driving passion was God's approval, he could be both gentle and forceful, depending on the situation. He walked in freedom.

Some people are afraid to be gentle. What might people think? Others are afraid to say the tough things. What might people think? Paul could defy people and confront leaders with great boldness because he did not fear their disapproval. If he addressed a hard topic and they didn't like it, he was not devastated. At the same time, Paul could be humble and gentle. He did not have to work at being impressive and powerful or go around comparing himself with other people to seem superior. He was comfortable in his own skin, free from anxiety about everyone's opinion of him. He was asking one question: "What will please God?"

**Read 2 Corinthians 10:1 – 2, 17 – 18; Galatians 1:10;
Acts 4:18 – 20; and Daniel 3:13 – 18**

3. How can focusing on God's approval free us to be bold, direct, and forceful in our relationships?

How can focusing on the approval of people get in the way of us expressing boldness and telling the hard truth in our relationships?

4. How can focusing on God's approval free us to be gentle and tender in our relationships?

How can focusing on the approval of people get in the way of us expressing gentleness and tenderness in our relationships?

5. What can help us decrease our need for the approval of people and focus more on the approval of God?

Taking Every Thought Captive

The writer David Burns notes that it is not other people's approval or compliments that make us feel good, but our belief that there is *validity* to what they say. I learned this lesson years ago in a very personal way when I did a summer internship at a mental health center. One female patient would regularly tell me that she wanted to marry me because she could not stop thinking about my body. You might think this would have flattered me, but the truth is that she was heavily medicated and said the very same thing to every other staff member and to some of the plants. Her compliment did nothing to enhance my sense of value as a person because I did not think it was valid and I gave it no power in my heart or life.

We think that when people approve of us they are making us feel good and when they disapprove of us they are making us feel bad, but that is not the case. No one's approval or disapproval can affect us unless we grant it credibility and status. This is why the apostle Paul could hear praise or critique and not let it dominate his life. He had learned to control his thoughts and gain a healthy perspective. Paul wrote, "We take captive every thought," and that is what each of us needs to do to be freed from the grip of approval addiction. We are involved in spiritual warfare. At least part of this business of taking every thought captive to Christ has to do with refusing to allow other people's approval or disapproval the power to dominate our life. The battle is not just in what others say to us or about us. Much of the battle is in our mind.

Read 2 Corinthians 10:3 – 6

6. How do you respond to *one* of the following statements?
   • It is not simply what people say that has power to encourage or discourage us. It is when we give validity to what they say that people have power in our life.

- Part of spiritual warfare is waged in the world of our thoughts. If we can control our thoughts, our lives can be transformed.

- It is possible to live free from the control and emotional roller coaster of other people's words and opinions of us.

7. What can we do to "take our thoughts captive" and break the power of approval addiction?

True and False Grounds for Approval

Paul's true ground for approval was a solid confidence that he belonged to Christ. Because he was crystal-clear about his identity, he had the strength to deal with criticism and conflict. Such should be the case in the heart of every follower of Jesus. We should be able to say, "I belong to Christ, what else really matters?" In comparison to knowing we are loved by God and belong to Jesus, the approval of people should pale in comparison.

Paul also addresses one of the false grounds for approval. It seems some of his detractors were saying that Paul's appearance was "unimpressive" and that he was not an effective communicator. Think about that. Paul was a preacher and people were saying, "We don't like to look at him or listen to him." Ouch! Sadly, these same false grounds for approval exist today. Many of us believe the cultural lie that we must look good and present ourselves well or we are not valuable. Paul learned what every Christian must embrace if we are to walk in freedom: our approval is secure in knowing that we belong to God through faith in Jesus. It is not based on how we look or perform in the eyes of each new critic that comes along.

Read 2 Corinthians 10:7 – 11; Romans 8:37 – 39; and 1 Samuel 16:7

8. What has helped you more fully understand that your value and approval are secure because you are a loved child of God?

What can erode your confidence in God's approval, and how do you fight against it?

9. How does our world make people feel "approved" or "disapproved" based on how we look and present ourselves?

What can we do to battle against the lie that our appearance dictates our value?

No Comparisons

Comparing ourselves to others has become a national pastime. We are obsessed with polls, surveys, and the most recent top-ten lists that tell us who are the richest, most powerful, best looking, or greatest. Into this pathologically comparison-oriented world, God speaks: "Just be who I have made you to be." The apostle Paul got this. He emphasized that comparing ourselves to others is a waste of time. If we have something to boast about, it should not be our accomplishments, but the great things of the Lord. If this truth can capture our hearts, we will experience great freedom to serve God and others.

Read 2 Corinthians 10:12 – 18

10. Comparing ourselves to others is dangerous. What are some of the possible harmful results if we compare ourselves to another person and feel they are better than us?

What are some of the possible harmful results if we compare ourselves to another person and feel we are better than them?

11. The apostle Paul says, "Let him who boasts boast in the Lord." What does it mean to boast in the Lord?

If you were to "boast in the Lord," what would you boast about?

Celebrating and Being Celebrated

In the book of Romans the apostle Paul wrote words that should help every follower of Christ live with a greater confidence that we do not have to be driven by the approval of others. Read this passage together as a group. If you feel comfortable doing so, you could even read in unison:

> What, then, shall we say in response to this? If God is for us, who can be against us? He who did not spare his own Son, but gave him up for us all—how will he not also, along with him, graciously give us all things? Who will bring any charge against those whom God has chosen? It is God who justifies. Who is he that condemns? Christ Jesus, who died—more than that, who was raised to life—is at the right hand of God and is also interceding for us. Who shall separate us from the love of Christ? Shall trouble or hardship or persecution or famine or nakedness or danger or sword? As it is written:

> "For your sake we face death all day long;
> we are considered as sheep to be slaughtered."

> No, in all these things we are more than conquerors through him who loved us. For I am convinced that neither death nor life, neither angels nor demons, neither the present nor the future, nor any powers, neither height nor depth, nor anything else in all creation, will be able to separate us from the love of God that is in Christ Jesus our Lord. (Romans 8:31–39)

Take time in prayer as a group thanking God for his love that creates security and strength.

Loving and Being Loved

Because our world can be brutal and make us feel that we do not measure up, it is important to be reminded that we are loved by God and find our approval in him. Take time in the coming week to meditate on the following passages. Read them, reflect deeply, and allow them to shape your view of who you are and where you find your sense of value.

- John 3:16–17
- 1 John 4:9–10
- Romans 5:8
- John 19–21

Serving and Being Served

When we are dominated by approval addiction we are not free to serve. But when we know who we are in Christ, refuse to compare ourselves to others, and boast only in the Lord, we are released to new levels of service. As you seek freedom from approval addiction, you will begin to identify places of service that never seemed possible before. As the Holy Spirit stirs new desires to serve, and fresh confidence that you could be fruitful in these areas in ministry, commit to respond and take a step forward for God's glory.

Serving in the Power of Weakness

2 CORINTHIANS 11:1–33

What does greatness look like? How do you recognize it? We each have our own list of people who were (or are) great in their particular field. In the corporate world we might identify examples like Bill Gates or Peter Drucker. In the realm of athletics names like Michael Jordan, Tiger Woods, Jackie Joyner-Kersee, and Lance Armstrong could be near the top of a very long list. Through the centuries people have been amazed by the gifts of artists such as van Gogh, Michelangelo, Beethoven, and Mozart. Just pick a category and "great people" come to mind.

But what does spiritual greatness look like? This seems to be a little more fluid and evasive. Maybe we could ask the question this way: What does greatness of spirit look like?

The dilemma comes as we realize that most standards of greatness in our world are not the guidelines God uses to determine greatness. In the kingdom of God things look very different. In a sense, they are almost upside down. Just think about it. Jesus said, "I tell you the truth: Among those born of women there has not risen anyone greater than John the Baptist" (Matthew 11:11). John served mostly in isolation and died young. What made him so great? It was his humility and willingness to point people to Jesus, not to himself. Jesus also taught, "Whoever wants to become great among you must be your servant, and whoever wants to be first must be slave of all" (Mark 10:43–44). As we read the Bible it becomes abundantly clear that God's path to greatness is dramatically different than the world's.

Making the Connection

1. Quickly jot down the names of people you think were (or are) great in some of the areas listed below:

   Sports:

   Business:

   Political Leadership:

   Music:

   Art:

   Literature:

   Science:

   What are some of the common characteristics that run through your list of "great people"?

Knowing and Being Known

Read 2 Corinthians 10:13 – 17 and 11:1 – 23

2. Paul is dealing with some leaders in the church who have brought with them a worldly view of greatness. He calls these people "super-apostles" or "false apostles." What marked the lives of these people?

3. The topic of boasting comes up often in these passages. What distinctions is Paul drawing between improper and proper boasting?

4. Paul drew clear distinctions between the tactics of the "super-apostles" and his own leadership style? What were the differences?

True Spiritual Greatness

Have you ever gotten so fed up with something that you just have to say what is on your mind? In that moment you are not thinking about how others will take it. This is the apostle Paul's state. He has heard enough of the super-apostles' bragging and boasting; has grown tired of all the reports of their strengths, gifts, and successes; has wearied of their flowing red capes and the giant "S" on their chests. The problem is that all the categories being used to measure these false apostles are worldly. Paul just has to speak to put things back into perspective. So he gives a list of his own "accomplishments," with the goal of giving a picture of true spiritual greatness.

Read 2 Corinthians 11:16–33; 12:7–10; and 1 Corinthians 1:26–31

5. Paul uses the word "boast" in a very different way than the super-apostles. He is clear that he is "speaking as a fool." In other words, he is trying to make a point. As you read this list of Paul's "accomplishments" in 2 Corinthians 11:21–30, what is the heartbeat of his boasting?

How do you think the super-apostles might have felt or responded to these words when Paul's letter arrived and was read in front of the congregation at Corinth?

6. At the heart of Paul's argument is the topic of weakness. Somehow, when we let go of our need to be powerful and in control, God's strength begins to flow into us. Paul declares, almost paradoxically, "For when I am weak, then I am strong" (2 Corinthians 12:10). Describe a time you came to the end of your strength and personal reserves and God showed up in power and carried you through.

7. Respond to *one* of the statements below:
   - Those who want to experience true spiritual greatness must embrace their weakness and look to God for his power.

   - When followers of Christ feel self-sufficient and able to minister in their own power ... beware!

   - True spiritual greatness looks radically different than any definition of greatness the world has ever espoused.

The Vulnerability of Love

Early twentieth-century sociologist Willard W. Waller once observed, "Among human beings, there is an inverse relationship between love and power. That is, in any relationship between two human beings, it is the person who has the greatest love that has the least power." If you don't believe this, just look at any dating couple. If one person is more interested in the relationship than the other, who has the upper hand? Who has the power? The one who is less in love. They call the shots.

This is the kind of weakness Paul is talking about when he says, "Who is weak, and I do not feel weak?" Paul has such love for the church that he feels vulnerable and weak. When there is a fight in the church, it breaks his heart. When a new believer stumbles back into sin, he weeps. When super-apostles show up and mislead the church, he is deeply troubled. Paul cares. He loves. And the willingness to love at this level puts him in a place of vulnerability. But love is always worth it.

Read 2 Corinthians 11:28–29

8. The weakness Paul is talking about is not a pathetic frailty but a mature willingness to love at a level that costs something, that commits to pour out self for the sake of others. Tell about a person in your life who has loved you at that level and was willing to be vulnerable and broken for your sake.

How did you see the love and power of Jesus in the actions of this person?

9. Who has God called you to love and serve at this level, and what step(s) can you take to show it?

10. Paul had a passionate love for the church — God's people gathered. How can we invest ourselves with vulnerable love in the local church?

"Boasting" in Weakness

When Paul says, "I will boast of the things that show my weakness," he is not saying, "I will boast about my emotional brokenness and neuroses." Certainly we all have our personal issues and we need to seek God's healing in these areas. In the church we need to create space where freedom and permission exists to work through our personal struggles. But this is not what Paul means when he speaks of boasting in weakness.

Consider for a moment the relationship between God and human beings. We usually think of God holding all the power, and of course, in many ways he does. He is sovereign, mighty, the creator and sustainer of all things, Lord over life and death, and the ultimate judge of humankind. He is on the throne ... always has been ... and always will be.

But there is a glorious sense in which God has chosen weakness, has chosen to love us with the deepest kind of love. While we might be fickle and our love can wander and wane, God's love does not. He loves his children tenaciously, jealously, passionately, and he will not let go. In a sense, he gives us power in the relationship: power to love or reject him. When human beings choose to reject God, it breaks his heart. If you don't believe this is a biblical image, read the book of Hosea. God is the most powerful being in the entire universe. Yet in his power, for our sake, he has chosen weakness.

Read 2 Corinthians 11:30 and 13:3 – 4

11. Reflect on the manger and the cross. How did God choose weakness for our sake?

What are ways we can choose weakness for God's sake, and for the sake of a world that needs to know the love of God?

Celebrating and Being Celebrated

Jesus modeled weakness over and over again during his journey on this earth. Indeed, his journey was one of intentional weakness: from the manger, to the upper room where he washed the disciples' feet, to the cross. The prophet Isaiah paints a picture of Jesus on the cross that describes not only his physical suffering but his spiritual work there:

> He was despised and rejected by men,
>   a man of sorrows, and familiar with suffering.
> Like one from whom men hide their faces
>   he was despised, and we esteemed him not.
> Surely he took up our infirmities
>   and carried our sorrows,
> yet we considered him stricken by God,
>   smitten by him, and afflicted.
> But he was pierced for our transgressions,
>   he was crushed for our iniquities;
> the punishment that brought us peace was upon him,
>   and by his wounds we are healed.
> We all, like sheep, have gone astray,
>   each of us has turned to his own way;
> and the LORD has laid on him
>   the iniquity of us all. (Isaiah 53:3–6)

Pray together as a group, thanking God for his willingness to become weak so that we might be healed. Ask the Holy Spirit to give you the courage to choose weakness when it will help others experience the presence and grace of God.

Loving and Being Loved

Take time to prayerfully reflect on the people in your life. Is there someone you know who God wants you to love and serve (it could be a spouse, child, parent, neighbor, or spiritual seeker), but you fear it will be too difficult or demand more than you want to give? Pray about this relationship. If you feel God wants you to extend vulnerable love, take the next step. If you don't feel you have all you need to care for this person, admit this to God and ask him to be strong for you in your place of weakness.

Serving and Being Served

The apostle Paul loved the church. He loved local congregations so much that it made him weak. He was willing to serve so faithfully that it cost him something. Today many people treat the church like a vendor of religious services. Their primary question when it comes to the church is, *What can I get from it?* It is time for followers of Christ to commit to give back.

If you are part of a local church and are not serving and giving, commit to find your place and begin investing. If you are not part of a local congregation, begin the process of finding a biblical community of believers and getting involved.

Session One — Messengers of Reconciliation
2 CORINTHIANS 2:5–17; 5:14–21

Question 1

Every one of us has been initiated into the "cause-and-effect program" of the world. The program is certainly obvious as we go to school and work for grades, or when some kids get lots of time on the sports field and others warm the bench. It can even be seen in Sunday school classes as children receive stars on a chart showing who has memorized the most Bible verses or attended the most weeks of the year. None of these things are inherently bad. They are just reminders that much of life is based on working hard to earn something. So when God introduces his "grace-plan," it can sound foreign, even a little questionable. Can it really be true that the greatest thing in the history of the world is offered for free?

Questions 2–3

From beginning to end, reconciliation is a gift offered by the grace of God. It is not earned ... it could not be. It is not deserved ... the Bible is clear that sinful people deserve judgment. This passage includes reminder after reminder of God's part in the work of reconciliation. It is God, in Christ, who makes us a new creation and does away with the old person. He is the One who was raised up and overcame the power of the grave. He is the One who reconciles us to the Father. It is God, in Christ, who chooses to no longer count our sins against us. Finally, we learn that the sinless Lamb of God became sin for us. Through his sacrifice we can become the righteousness of God.

When we become ambassadors of reconciliation, we are simply pointing to the One who has already done all of the work. As we receive this amazing gift and point others toward the author of salvation, we are doing our part. We can't reconcile people, we can't forgive people, and we can't change people ... only

God can do this. Our part is joyfully accepting what God has offered freely to us and then telling others that they too can be reconciled to a loving God.

Questions 4–5

Isaiah 52–53, written centuries before Jesus lived, is a prophetic prefiguring of what he would suffer when he went to the cross to die in our place for our sins. Second Corinthians is written on the other side of the cross, after Jesus has suffered, died, and risen again. Paul is reminding us of the powerful reality of Christ's death and how we have died with him. This means we are also raised with Jesus and live each day for his glory and in the power of his resurrection.

Question 6

It is not bragging to say, "I have been changed by the power of Jesus." God's Word tells us that we are being transformed from an old person to a new person. With this in mind we should feel comfortable talking about the change God is making in us. Old attitudes of prejudice, hatred, and resentment are being purged. Our hearts and lives begin to reflect grace, love, and forgiveness. Fear is being replaced by confidence and trust. Lust is being supplanted by a hunger for purity. Impatience is waning and understanding is becoming the order of the day. It can't be stopped. In Christ we are becoming a new creation. As this happens, we can joyfully share our stories of God's power in us, transforming our lives.

Question 7

When the apostle Paul says that followers of Christ will bring the "smell of death" he is acknowledging a simple spiritual truth. Not everyone we meet will like how we smell. In other words, Christians who follow Christ passionately can be a nuisance in this world. We shine light in dark places, and some people want to stay in the dark. We speak truth into falsehood. The very message we bring is offensive to some because they are spiritually dead and we come with a message of life.

This is why people who are steeped in immorality are bothered when we talk about holiness. It is why people who advocate sexual promiscuity take offense at those who believe God has set clear boundaries for sexual expression. It is why those who live in excess and hedonistic pursuit of pleasure are upset by Christians who follow a higher power than their own desires and whims. To those who know Jesus and are part of his family, other believers smell good. To those who are running from God and pursuing their own desires, we might just smell like death.

Question 8

Because all of us have been raised with a sense that we get what we earn and earn what we get, it is easy to carry over this mind-set to our faith. If we do, we end up with errant theology. When it comes to reconciliation with God, there is nothing we can do to earn it and nothing we can add to the work of Christ on the cross. If we are going to live in grace and be effective ambassadors of God's reconciling message, we must let go of any sense that we earn, deserve, or merit it. All we can do is receive what God has already accomplished, be deeply thankful, and share it freely with others.

Questions 9–11

Ambassadors live in another country in order to be representatives of their homeland. In the same way, every follower of Christ is called to live as an ambassador. We are not to cloister ourselves away in a closed circle of Christians but to be in the world as messengers of reconciliation.

Too many followers of Christ get so invested in the church and Christian activities that they sever all ties with those who are not yet in God's family. It is time for each of us to evaluate our life and schedule to make sure we have regular and healthy contacts with people outside the Christian bubble. As we do, we can fulfill God's call to live as ambassadors of his grace.

Session Two — The Power of Endurance
2 CORINTHIANS 1:3–7; 4:7–18; 6:3–10; 11:16–29

Question 1

God is at work even in and through our sufferings. He stands at our side and says, "Don't quit. Keep going." Moms of young children need to hear this call to endurance. Day after day they face the same routine, change the same kind of diapers, wash the same dishes, and wipe the same runny noses. They have almost no "me" time anymore, and are often so tired and isolated that they feel like they are not growing spiritually. These heroes need to be reminded that the kingdom of God is found in the midst of the routine and the energy-draining demands of ordinary life.

No matter whether we're students or office workers, short-order cooks or optometrists, we can all feel like what we do each day is mundane, routine, and unimportant. But God cheers us on. If we are fulfilling his plans and purposes for our life, no matter how ordinary they might seem, God whispers, "Hang in there. Don't give up. Endure. It will all be worth it."

Questions 2–3

These two passages offer a staggering list of suffering, heartache, hardship, and pain. When we realize Paul was a real man facing real situations, it are almost too hard to hear. Yet his endurance and the attitude he maintained through every trial is a glorious example for every follower of Christ. His sufferings help us put things in perspective and inspire us to evaluate how we respond to the battles we face.

If Paul could sit and listen to some of the "prosperity" and "health and wealth" preachers of our day, I'm sure he would take them to task and challenge the very fabric of their teaching and ministry. Yes, Paul taught that God loves his children and offers good gifts; he believed God's favor is real and those who walk with Jesus are the most blessed people on this earth. But he would vigorously disagree with the underpinnings of any theological teaching that claims that good Christians never suffer or struggle.

Paul taught the exact opposite. When a follower of Jesus lives by faith and follows the Savior, suffering is part of the deal. All we have to do is look at the example of Jesus. He followed the will of the Father and ended up despised, rejected, falsely accused, and nailed to a cross.

Questions 4–6

Just like Paul, each of us faces our own set of hardships in this life, some small and some larger. Some are facing financial or vocational pressures that feel oppressive. Others are in a marriage or a relationship that is causing intense difficulty. Some are struggling with an addictive sin and not sure how they are going to overcome it. Some, like Paul, are facing unrelenting criticism that makes them want to crawl into a hole and hide. Some are experiencing intense physical pain and wonder how they will hang on another day. No matter what we face, we need to be reminded that the greatest spiritual victories on this planet come when people simply endure, holding tightly to the hand of God. As we press on with full integrity and sincerity, we become more mature, closer to the heart of God, and more like Jesus.

It is helpful for us to hear a qualifying statement at this point. The call to endure does not mean that whatever situation we find ourselves in will last forever. In Acts 12 an angel comes to deliver Peter, who had been imprisoned by Herod. When the angel says, "Follow me," Peter does not respond by saying, "No, I'm staying here because prison can be a good learning experience." He follows the angel and gets out.

There is a time to walk away. If you are in an abusive work situation, it might be time to find a new job. If you are in a relationship that is doing massive damage, the call to endurance does not mean you never walk away. We also have to use wisdom, asking the Spirit for discernment. To quote the musical theologian Kenny Rogers, "You gotta know when to hold 'em, know when to fold 'em, know when to walk away, know when to run." There is nothing noble or Christ-honoring about staying in an unhealthy situation when God is not calling us to endure.

The call to endure, at its heart, is the call to hold fast to Christ. It is not about suffering for suffering's sake. It is the call to hold fast to those commitments that you must honor if you are going to be a Christ follower. It is hard. But it is often the way of obedience.

Questions 7–9

These two words—"light" and "momentary"—can change our lives. When we get the perspective of eternity and see things through kingdom lenses, everything looks different.

When your boss hassles you, you can say "light" and "momentary." When your kids leave a bike under the rear tires of the car and you hear it crunch as you back out of the driveway, you can say "light" and "momentary." When your car is stuck in a snow drift and you have to hike through sub-zero wind chills to get help, you can say "light" and "momentary." Paul faced far worse — persecution, beatings, imprisonment, dishonor, poverty, sorrow, death — and used the same two adjectives to describe them all: "light" and "momentary."

Questions 10–11

At the end of the day, the benefits of endurance do not only lie in eternity. There is fruit today. Paul actually begins the letter to the church at Corinth with a powerful reminder that our moments of pain and hardship become a training ground. When we have experienced the comfort and ministry of God's presence in our times of sorrow and struggle, he can use us, if we're willing, to minister to others who face similar pain.

Session Three — Pure Life
2 CORINTHIANS 6:14–7:1

Question 1

The Bible would say that the importance of the purity of our food pales in comparison to the issue of the purity of the human heart. We should share God's concern for holiness and purity. Even though the world uses a sliding scale, we should not. As followers of Christ our standards should match those set by God. This does not mean we condemn ourselves or the world every time we fall short of God's standards. If we did this, we would live in perpetual condemnation. Instead, it means we stay profoundly aware of God's purity standards and strive to live lives that will reflect his presence and bring honor to his name.

Questions 2–3

Paul uses very strong language to talk about this business of purity. To understand why Paul writes so strongly, almost harshly, we must understand the culture of Corinth. Paul is addressing a very specific situation with some very severe challenges to purity. As you saw in the "Welcome to Corinth" section, it was a place of unparalleled hedonism in the ancient world. The love of money and the religious and sexual perversity of Corinth were known far and wide.

In addition to this, a brief geography lesson might also be helpful. Greece was divided into two parts, and Corinth was in a very narrow slip of land right in the middle. That meant that all of the land commerce that went north and south in Greece had to travel through Corinth. Beyond that fact, Greece sat in the Mediterranean region and ships traveling from Europe to Asia, or vice versa, would travel via Corinth and its connecting isthmus to avoid the more stormy and dangerous waters to the south. So Corinth was always filled with sailors, business people, travelers, and all sorts of pleasure seekers. It was a culture that placed a high value on entertainment and luxury. If you were looking for any pleasure that the ancient world had to offer, and if you had some money in your pocket, you would find what you wanted in Corinth.

Questions 4–5

The most powerful antidote to impurity is the presence of God. If we are going to grow in purity and avoid that which will make us impure, we need to walk each day hand in hand with God. An awareness of God's presence with us helps us see with his eyes, hear with his ears, feel with his heart, and make decisions based on what will honor him. Most kids curtail bad behavior when Dad or Mom is around. But when they are alone, they make very different choices. If we can live each day with a sense that our loving, compassionate, holy Father is with us, this will shape so many of our choices. (The accountability of a small group can also help in this regard.)

Part of the way we can do this is by finding time, each day, when we can pay particular attention to the voice and presence of God. Of course, we want to experience God's intimacy at every moment, but this is developed as we set aside quality time alone with him. I tend to be a morning person so I make it a holy habit to meet with God early in the day, and this builds my connection with him for the rest of the day. For others, lunch break or the evening might be a great quality time. The issue is not so much *when* but *that* we develop a pattern of making space for God each day.

Paul is saying, "Ultimately, you choose between one of two trajectories; toward God and life or away from God and toward death." He is saying, "Once you have chosen God, don't do anything to put yourself back on that old trajectory ... it leads to death. Don't make a commitment to a deep relationship that you know is going to pull you away from God. Be careful who you allow yourself to be yoked to."

Throughout the history of the church the single most important relationship that falls under Paul's discussion of being equally yoked has been marriage. When I was going into my third year of graduate school, I went on a blind date with a woman named Nancy, who is now my wife. At the end of the date we talked about our life plans and dreams. I had never talked to someone where there was such an immediate shared connection about life, God, and a passion for ministry. With time this similar vision led us to become yoked together.

Those who get into a yoked relationship with someone who is not a follower of Christ may find themselves being pulled away from God. Even if that doesn't happen, the fact remains that the person who is closest to you in this world cannot share your greatest dreams and loves. If Nancy were not a believer, I believe that I would still be committed to loving and honoring God, but there are so many moments that I would have lost because we would not see things from the same perspective.

Paul says, "Don't be unequally yoked." This statement could be painful for some reading this study guide. Some are single, and would like very much to get married. It is hard enough to find somebody who is sane and healthy, much less a passionate follower of Jesus. But it is better to wait than to jump into a relationship where you are yoked to someone who might lead you away from everything that matters most to you.

For others these words are painful because you are already married to somebody who is not a follower of Christ. You need to recognize that the intimacy you so deeply crave will be fully satisfied by God alone. And you need to keep loving your spouse, praying for them, and asking God to draw their heart to him so that one day the two of you will walk side by side, yoked together in Jesus.

Questions 8–9

Because God wants us to be pure and holy, he is very serious about what we touch. In contrast, our culture has adopted a "touch everything" mentality. It is critical that every follower of Christ learn how to identify what is clean and unclean in their life. The challenge is that clean and unclean can be a moving target. Some things are always unclean. For example, it is never right and purity-enhancing for a Christian to handle pornography.

There are also things that might be unclean at one point in your life and clean at another time. Or, there are things that might be unclean for one person but clean for another. One example is a TV remote control. If TV consumption is keeping someone from walking closely with God, the remote is an unclean thing. But, at another time or in the hands of a different person, it might not be unclean. This is why we need to be prayerful and responsive to the Holy Spirit as we identify the unclean things we should not touch.

Questions 10–11

In some ways it might be easier to just go live in a cave, to run away from the world and all of its enticements. But God calls us to be salt and light, to be *in* this world but not shaped *by* it. This does not come easily. It involves great wisdom and occasionally withdrawing from specific circumstances or places that we know will lead to impurity in our lives. But, as God's people, we are to stay in the world and make an impact for Jesus.

Session Four – Gracious Generosity
2 CORINTHIANS 8:1–12

Question 1

Our culture does not overtly call money or possessions a god. We don't refer to those who live for the accumulation of material things an "idolater." But if we were to say that a person worships what they love most and spend the most time pursuing and talking about, we would have to admit that many people worship what Jesus called "Mammon." They invest all they have into the acquisition and care of stuff. Sadly, our culture doesn't see this as odd or wrong, rather as a character quality to be praised.

Questions 2–3

The Corinthian church members were fairly recent converts living in a market-driven, materialistic hub of the world. Their environment was quite a bit like ours today.

The Greek province of Macedonia had several different churches, among them the one in Philippi. Paul writes about them living in a severe ordeal of affliction. He says that the Macedonians were characterized by two traits: a remarkably high level of joy and a deep level of poverty. Many people would say that the term "joyful poverty" is an oxymoron. But Paul did not see it this way and neither did the Macedonian believers.

When Paul started his ministry, controversy abounded over his bringing the gospel to the Gentiles. Some people within the original church, made up of Jewish converts to Christianity, did not want to extend the gospel to non-Jews. Finally, a church council in Jerusalem decided to affirm his work among Gentiles (Acts 15). In the process they gave Paul a special word of instruction: "All they asked was that we should continue to remember the poor, the very thing I [Paul] was eager to do" (Galatians 2:10). From the beginning, gracious generosity was central to the gospel. As Paul traveled to Gentile regions and started churches he was commissioned to raise funds to help support the poor believers in Jerusalem.

A great cultural barrier existed in Paul's day between Gentile and Jewish people. For the most part they despised each other and avoided all contact. But God was building a bridge . . . right in the middle of the church. As Paul traveled he invited Gentile believers to give graciously and generously to help support the Jewish poor in Jerusalem. It is this special collection that the believers in Macedonia got so excited about participating in. This project had tremendous significance, for it was a visible expression of the fact that Jesus had torn down what he called "the wall of hostility" between Jew and Gentile. It is yet today a tangible sign of the oneness in the body of Christ.

Questions 4–5

These equations look foreign and strange at first glance. But when we reflect a little more deeply, we realize that heavenly economics are different than earthly financial equations.

> Abundant Joy + Extreme Poverty = A Wealth of Generosity
> Discontent + Extreme Affluence = A Famine of Generosity

Most people would think that those with more money might be the most generous, but in fact people with higher levels of joy are the most liberal givers. The point is, people with either very limited resources or very great resources can be extremely generous. When they know the grace of God and experience real inner joy, giving follows. On the other hand, a rich or poor person can be equally stingy and selfish.

Questions 6–7

How do people give beyond their means? It involves God enlarging their capacity to give more than they could do on their own. God did this for the Macedonian believers. The apostle Paul talks about this same thing in both 2 Corinthians 8:3 and 9:11–12. Explaining what happens when we begin to give, he says, "You will be made rich in every way so that you can be generous on every occasion, and through us your generosity will result in thanksgiving to God" (9:11). The idea is that generosity opens a flood of provision from God. In a sense, he is stewarding resources to a person because he knows they will be quick to pass them on to serve others.

When people's hearts become captivated by the desire to give, God enables them to give in ways they could not have anticipated. Their lives become adventures in giving and they overflow with joy. That's why the Christians of Macedonia, despite their poverty, begged earnestly for the grace, or privilege, of sharing in the ministry of helping the poor in Jerusalem.

Questions 8–9

The apostle Paul draws all kinds of connections between grace and generosity. Out of the gracious heart of the Father, his love propelled him to send his only Son. It is the grace of Jesus that gives us the chance to be forgiven and know the hope of heaven. In response, it is the grace of God alive in us that moves us to be like Jesus and share what we have with others. This is evidenced by the Macedonian believers who were so overwhelmed with God's grace that they begged for the chance to give to people in need. It seems that grace moves us to generous giving, and learning to give with generosity helps us understand grace more fully.

Questions 10–11

From beginning to end the story of Jesus turns our human expectations on its head. His kingdom was upside down in most every way. If you want to be great, become a servant (and Jesus washed the feet of his followers). If you want to be first, choose to be last (and Jesus died on a cross between two common thieves). Jesus left the riches of heaven to take on the rags of human flesh.

He loved the outcast. He touched lepers. He reached out to the hated tax collectors and shared meals with the most notorious of sinners. The king of heaven did not come to wear a crown of gold, but a crown of thorns. He did not sit on a throne, but was lifted up on a cross. In every way possible, Jesus humbled himself and served. What an example for all who call themselves his followers!

Session Five – The Right Motivation for Serving
2 CORINTHIANS 10:1–18

Question 1

Approval addiction is common because it is woven into the fabric of culture. From childhood most of us learn that we get more praise, affirmation, and even love if we "behave." We are taught to care what others think about us. "What will the neighbors think?" is a classic question that reveals this concern. In many homes one of the driving forces to motivate children is the need to be "popular," "liked," and "included." In most cases, we don't even see the desire to be approved of as a bad thing. And, on some levels, it is not bad. We don't want to go through life having no regard for what anyone else thinks. But, when we are driven and motivated by the approval of people and not the desire to please God, we get into all sorts of trouble.

Question 2

Paul had been to a large extent liberated from approval addiction. He lived with a longing for the commendation of God and was not driven by a need for the praise of people. Because of this he was free to speak the truth in love: to confront people when they needed it and to be gentle when appropriate.

In this portion of 2 Corinthians, Paul is beginning a new section of his letter to the Corinthian believers. From here to the end of the book he will be hitting some tough topics with a lot of force and boldness. One of those topics is the presence of false teachers or false apostles in the church who were trying to promote disunity by promoting a different gospel. They were trying to tear down Paul's credibility as an apostle and a teacher, saying that Paul was not impressive personally, not attractive physically, and not dynamic as a communicator.

Paul was under heavy criticism. He was not about to avoid confrontation, because the health of the community was at stake. On the other hand, he didn't want to use his position as a teacher to overwhelm or crush people. What you see in this chapter is a masterful guide, a bit of instruction, about dealing with conflict and confrontation.

Questions 3–5

Paul, like Jesus, is living under the gracious approval of God. He doesn't need to placate people. He doesn't need to power up on people or throw his weight around. He doesn't need to compete. At the same time, he can stand up to the most powerful and intimidating forces of his day. Paul faced political pressure, social pressure, religious pressure — people at the top of the religious hierarchy and the Roman government. He stood up to them all and did not bat an eye. He was not worried because he knew the approval and commendation of the Father ... and that is always enough. Paul is a beautiful picture of what it looks like to have been liberated from approval addiction.

We all will face times when people will try to leverage acceptance and approval to get us to jump through their hoops. If we can live free of the need for this kind of human applause, we can spend our days doing what God wants, not chasing the latest whims of others.

Questions 6–7

Between other people's approval and our pleasure in it is our assessment of the validity of their beliefs. We are not passive victims of other people's opinions. In fact, their opinions are powerless until we validate them.

Paul lives a different kind of life than his opponents and that enables him to live under the approval of God and be liberated from the need to get it from other people. Paul says what we face in these moments is nothing less than spiritual warfare, an inner battle for our hearts and minds. He says we must assess our thoughts and beliefs to make sure we are not living a lie. We can disarm the influence of other people if we commit, with God's help, to not allow them to have power over us: that their approval will not direct our life nor will their disapproval dominate our choices or manipulate us.

Questions 8–9

Paul is clear that we fortify our souls and are equipped to resist approval addiction when we know that our identity is established by who we are in Christ. If we can become single-minded in our awareness of the love, favor, and grace of God, the need for human approval dissolves.

On the other hand, we must also identify and reject the lies of culture that our value is found in how we look and the impression we can make on others. Many of us have felt the anguish of being told we do not meet up with whatever standards of physical desirability society puts in place. Others of us feel like physical attractiveness is about all we have to offer and lean on. Either scenario is a prison from which God wants to free us. If we are still basing our sense of worth and value on how we look, it is time to see ourselves as beautiful in the eyes of God and let that be enough.

Questions 10 – 11

God wants us to live free from the need to compare ourselves to others. Someone once said:

- When people are in their twenties they live to please others and think a lot about their opinions.
- When they are in their thirties they get tired of trying to please others and get mad at them instead.
- When they are in their forties they realize nobody was thinking about them the whole time and wonder why they spent so much focusing on the opinions of others.

Sadly, it seems many people in their fifties and beyond are still living with the need for approval. God wants to set us free from the comparison game. We can't help it if people compare themselves to us, but we do not have to compare ourselves to them. We do not have to spend one more day investing our energies into trying to be better than someone else. Instead, we can pour our passions and strength into giving God glory and serving him and others. When we do this, motivated by a desire to please God, our service is sweet and our joy is full.

Session Six – Serving in the Power of Weakness
2 CORINTHIANS 11:1 – 33

Questions 2 – 4

As you read this portion of 2 Corinthians you find that the word "boast" comes up over and over again (10:13, 14, 15, 16, 17; 11:10, 12, 16, 17, 18, 21, 30; see also 12:1 – 6). Paul's opponents, the super-apostles, are threatening not only the unity of the church but also the Corinthians' understanding of the gospel. Chapters 10 – 13 reveal a fundamental disagreement over how to recognize the presence and the work of God. The issue at hand is what constitutes spiritual greatness.

Paul's opponents (and we have to read between the lines to get the full story) are into what might be called a "theology of glory." They are impressive guys who are self-promoters and wield a lot of power. Their greatness is obvious and intimidating.

Paul, by contrast, is not an impressive guy. He suffers often and he suffers deeply, and his missions sometimes end in failure. He is into what has been called "a theology of the cross." Instead of flaunting his authority, he lives a life of servanthood.

The truth is, from the perspective of the kingdom of God, the greatest people are the least boastful, the least invested in self-promotion. That is as true today as it was in Paul's.

Questions 5–7

When Paul begins to talk about boasting it almost looks as if he is going to play the same game as the super-apostles, but he is not. That is why Paul says, "I'm talking like a fool." Here is the twist: the super-apostles are boasting about how great they are (again, reading between the lines). They are wonderful speakers, have impressive presence, possess powerful gifts. Paul says, "Okay, let me boast." But he does not boast about his strength, good looks, accomplishments, or successful ministry. He does something very different.

Paul boasts about suffering, about pain, about failure. He says, "If what you are looking for is a glamorous, triumphant, success-crowned ministry, take a look at this: I have been beaten, flogged, imprisoned, stoned, shipwrecked, hungry, thirsty, and exhausted."

He concludes the chapter (11:32–33) with a story of humiliation, reminding the people of one of the most demeaning moments in his life. The man who had once been known as the mighty Saul was now the humbled Paul. He had once gone from city to city authorized by the highest leaders of Israel to persecute the church. Now he had been relegated to a Christian preacher who was on the run and had to be secretly lowered out of a window in the wall of the city in a basket ... like a load of dirty laundry. What a contrast to the the super-apostles' stories.

The super-apostles came to Corinth to proclaim another gospel and another Jesus. Paul warns the Corinthians, "Don't let these people make slaves of you or take advantage of you." The idea here is that these super-apostles were exploiting the people of Corinth for personal gain. They were sponging off the people. Paul wanted to be able to proclaim the gospel boldly with no strings attached, so he accepted no money from the church while he was there.

Remember, there were no printing presses in those days. When Paul's letter arrived in Corinth it would have been normative for someone to read it to the gathered congregation. Just imagine the super-apostles sitting there as Paul's letter was read. No doubt at some points they were angered and frustrated. At other points they might have become defensive and wanted to explain their position. Hopefully some experienced brokenness and repentance.

Questions 8–10

Love leads to vulnerability and weakness. Biblical weakness that comes as a by-product of authentic love is not about being a pushover or a doormat. It is weakness in the strongest sense, the kind that leads a person to willingly suffer, endure pain, and sacrifice for those they love. This is what Paul did, what Jesus did, and it is how we are called to live. When we see the face of Jesus as he suffered for us, we know that loving is more important than avoiding pain.

Question 11

Paul says Jesus was crucified in weakness. What does this mean? It means that Jesus *embraced* suffering and pain. He remained on the cross even when people taunted him with such words as "He saved others, he cannot save himself." What they didn't realize was that when they thought Jesus was at his weakest he was actually displaying the ultimate demonstration of God's power. When we get this, we willingly follow Jesus, even into weakness.

The way of Christ is to choose the pursuit of love over the avoidance of pain. Such thinking is countercultural, foreign to the world, but it is at the very heart of the gospel. As we grow to understand the manger, cross, and ministry of Jesus, we are led to places of humble, sacrificial service that can only be accomplished in the power of God.

WILLOW
Willow Creek Association

Willow Creek Association
Vision, Training, Resources for Prevailing Churches

This resource was created to serve you and to help you build a local church that prevails. It is just one of many ministry tools that are part of the Willow Creek Resources® line, published by the Willow Creek Association together with Zondervan.

The Willow Creek Association (WCA) was created in 1992 to serve a rapidly growing number of churches from across the denominational spectrum that are committed to helping unchurched people become fully devoted followers of Christ. Membership in the WCA now numbers over 12,000 Member Churches worldwide from more than ninety denominations.

The Willow Creek Association links like-minded Christian leaders with each other and with strategic vision, training, and resources in order to help them build prevailing churches designed to reach their redemptive potential. Here are some of the ways the WCA does that.

- **The Leadership Summit**—a once a year, two-and-a-half-day conference to envision and equip Christians with leadership gifts and responsibilities. Presented live at Willow Creek as well as via satellite broadcast to over 130 locations across North America, this event is designed to increase the leadership effectiveness of pastors, ministry staff, volunteer church leaders, and Christians in the marketplace.

- **Ministry-Specific Conferences**—throughout each year the WCA hosts a variety of conferences and training events—both at Willow Creek's main campus and offsite, across the U.S., and around the world—targeting church leaders and volunteers in ministry-specific areas such as: small groups, preaching and teaching, the arts, children, students, volunteers, stewardship, etc.

- **Willow Creek Resources®**—provides churches with trusted and field-tested ministry resources in such areas as leadership, evangelism, spiritual formation, spiritual gifts, small groups, stewardship, student ministry, children's ministry, the use of the arts—drama, media, contemporary music—and more.

- **WCA Member Benefits**—includes substantial discounts to WCA training events, a 20 percent discount on all Willow Creek Resources®, *Defining Moments* monthly audio journal for leaders, quarterly *Willow* magazine, access to a Members-Only section on WillowNet, monthly communications, and more. Member Churches also receive special discounts and premier services through WCA's growing number of ministry partners—Select Service Providers—and save an average of $500 annually depending on the level of engagement.

For specific information about WCA conferences, resources, membership, and other ministry services contact:

Willow Creek Association
P.O. Box 3188
Barrington, IL 60011-3188
Phone: 847-570-9812
Fax: 847-765-5046
www.willowcreek.com

Share Your Thoughts

With the Author: Your comments will be forwarded to
the author when you send them to *zauthor@zondervan.com*.

With Zondervan: Submit your review of this book
by writing to *zreview@zondervan.com*.

Free Online Resources at
www.zondervan.com/hello

 Zondervan AuthorTracker: Be notified whenever your favorite authors publish new books, go on tour, or post an update about what's happening in their lives.

 Daily Bible Verses and Devotions: Enrich your life with daily Bible verses or devotions that help you start every morning focused on God.

 Free Email Publications: Sign up for newsletters on fiction, Christian living, church ministry, parenting, and more.

 Zondervan Bible Search: Find and compare Bible passages in a variety of translations at www.zondervanbiblesearch.com.

 Other Benefits: Register yourself to receive online benefits like coupons and special offers, or to participate in research.